T0380941

FINAL AFRICAN PAPERS
OF
SIMON
OTTENBERG

To order additional copies of this book, contact:
Xlibris
844-714-8691
www.Xlibris.com
Orders@Xlibris.com

ISBN: 978-1-6698-7143-9 (sc)
ISBN: 978-1-6698-7144-6 (hc)
ISBN: 978-1-6698-7142-2 (e)

Library of Congress Control Number: 2023905232

Print information available on the last page

Rev. date: 04/10/2023

Contents

Random Thoughts on Afikpo and Igbo Culture and Society

I carried out research with an eastern Igbo group, the Afikpo, in 1952–1953 and 1959–1960 with shorter trips up through 2010, and although I have attempted to follow Igbo events since then, my comments here largely grow out of my two extensive research periods among the Igbos. I have deliberately omitted my footnotes; this is my knowledge and experience.

History

The earliest Igbo settlement was in the Awka-Nri region hundreds of years ago when, later on, a small Igbo state arose for a short time. Before these events, there was an immense expansion of the Igbos to the west, across the Niger River; to the east, to the western borders of Cross River; to the north, to the Nsukka region; and they moved to just north of the later emerging coastal slave-trading towns with whom the Igbos traded in slaves that were obtained by slave-raiding groups in the interior.

Igbo expansion wiped out, absorbed, or pushed aside small hunting and agricultural groups that had existed in the conquered region. The Igbos came with superior technologies and greater numbers.

A similar movement east of the Igbo, of a considerable number of technologically superior people, left the Cameroon ridge and moved westward to the east side of the Cross River while also overcoming peoples with elemental technologies and agriculture. The movement involved numerous different linguistic and ethnic groups that were non-Igbo.

These movements, those of the Igbo and those from the Cameroons, and the growth of the coastal towns essentially shaped the culture and the political economy of southeastern Nigeria together with a few other smaller ethnic groups in the region, such as the Ibibio and the Ogoni.

Boys in Training

Early childhood training may have been a factor in Igbo culture, as the emphasis was placed both on boys' independence and group cooperation. Boys stopped living with their mothers at about the age of five and began residing in a special house in the compound, forming or, more likely, joining an independent boy's group. If a boy saw little of his mother he saw less of his father, father, who lived in his own house and may have had other wives to attend to, at this time. Each compound, and there might be ten or more compounds in a village, had such a boy's house. These boys played competitive games that were passed down from generation to generation and created new ones. They engaged in all varieties of sexual acts on themselves and other boys. They lived this way until they were initiated in their teens into the village men's secret society. In some Afikpo villages, boys had to previously perform a test alone in front of the village secret society members. This act was, at times, rehearsed with the father. This form of childhood training might have led to high achievement.

Achievement

The Igbos have a reputation for being high achievers in southeastern Nigeria. They have been considered by some other

Nigerians as being extremely aggressive in whatever activity they are engaged in, whether it be in business, politics, sports, modern fiction, music, or poetry. This assertiveness in life is believed to have characterized both Igbo individuals and the groups of the Igbo. They are thought by others to be preoccupied with success. The Igbos believe this to be so, pointing out examples of their achievements. Nigerians who are not Igbos believe this to be true as well. The fact is nobody has seriously proven the existence of a high level of achievement, whether it is true or not is not known. It may be a social illusion that has grown out of Igbo interrelationships with other Nigerian ethnic groups. However, let us accept that they are openly assertive, hard working people, that other ethnic groups may also have important assertive qualities, and what may be a social misconception is true. Both the Igbo and non-Igbo can cite cases of Igbo success, so perhaps it is true.

There were numerous explanations for Igbo achievement. Other Nigerian cultures in Africa are also achievers. This achievement level partially depended on the external situation in which the cultural groups found themselves at a particular time. For the Igbos, it was during the precolonial history of continual expansions due to population growth, land shortages, and superior technology over those people they conquered. For hundreds of years, the Igbos pushed away or absorbed other ethnic groups at their borders to form an increasingly larger Igbo cultural area before colonialism stabilized the Igbo borders. These expansions must have required high achievement levels and often met resistance from other cultures.

The colonial and postcolonial situation allowed for further movement of the Igbos, within Nigeria and to Europe and America. All these external movements can be seen as the consequences of strong economic needs. Thus, it is likely that traditional childhood experience and population pressures leading to geographic mobility have both been linked to Igbo achievement and motivation in the past.

A question to which we have no answer is what were the factors that led to the Igbo's superior technology over the existing aboriginal peoples in the Awka region? Near the later development of a small religious state at Nri, what were the factors in the Awka region that led to the Igbos developing superior technology? How will we find out?

Since colonial days in Nigeria until the present, Igbo achievement has been hampered by Igbo styles of decision-making. Decision making at Igbo meetings often took a long time, and on occasion in the past, matters were only settled through consultation with the spiritual forces inside or outside the community. The Igbos could very well maintain their high level of vocalization without losing their momentum. But multiple voices in decision-making did not make for easily reached decisions. Both the process of swearing the truth at a special Igbo swear shrine to declare their innocence, and consulting an oracle have been employed to finalize matters. Individualism and achievement have occurred within a social structure and controlled its direction within that structure through social breaks in the system in terms of an occasional dominance of a palaver man in discussion by the elders, or the separation of lineages or village parts, but they were soon adjusted to without great difficulty except in the dispute between Ndibe and Anohia Nkalo communities, which was long-standing.

It was different for females in the traditional Afikpo society. Achievement meant successfully producing children for the husband and growing enough farm crops beyond the family's needs to sell and have little to spend. It also meant having personal leadership skills to direct women's activities and to maintain the spiritual wall between men and women. Women feared the spirits men controlled, and thus, they feared or were ambivalent toward male priests. In any case, the possibilities for women's achievement were limited in the real world of Afikpo until the end of colonialism.

Igbo Qualities

The Igbos' early aggressive expansion may relate to their reputation as high achievers today. They are communicative and direct in talking, including by cell phone and email. They are individuals who are willing to express their ideas and views publicly. They enjoy argument and debate. Despite their high level of Western education in Igboland, Igbo life is strongly oral. Discussion and disagreement are endemic. Vocal enthusiasm is related to traditional Igbo social life and its indigenous Igbo political systems, which stressed group meetings to reach a consensus with an emphasis on skillful speech and the frequent use of proverbs, verbal analogy, and metaphor.

The Afikpo Town Welfare Association

In the 1950s, as independence was approaching, each Igbo village group established welfare associations to uplift their group. In Afikpo it was the Afikpo Town Welfare association such as the Afikpo Town Welfare Association, popularly known as ATWA. The majority of its members living at Afikpo had some Western education. It had branches in major cities where sufficient members existed. The branches consisted of salaried workers, having greater resources than the home ATWA, funding such projects as the improvement of the Afikpo water supply and school scholarships.

But the history of the various collapses in both the home

organization and some branches, with accusations of major thefts of funds and rivalries among members that should not have occurred suggested problems with self-authority among educated Afikpo. The problem was the lack of authority and the lack of traditional religious support, such as the swearing of innocence at a spirit shrine or consulting an oracle, but the educated Igbo rejected such methods.

Girls and Women

Since colonialism, there have been remarkable changes in the Igbo female situation. They flocked to schools by the 1960s, and there are more women in some colleges and universities in Nigeria than men. They are into teaching, including university teaching. They have started and run furniture and other businesses. They are in politics and are now internationally known for their novels as well.

Withdrawal

The distinguished Igbo historian, Professor Adiele Afigbo,

has pointed out to me that the very strength of Igbo individuals' achievement has meant that unity among the Igbo frequently has failed in local, regional, and national affairs. Igbos have tended to break up into factions, and for autonomous communities to develop. There have been failures of the Igbo to provide something like a united front in the face of external pressures from the rest of Nigeria, except during the Biafran War.(I am aware that all of this is also true to some extent of other Nigerian cultural groups, such as the Yoruba.) I have noted that the Igbo are vocal and often direct, but this does not always lead to compromise or to coming up with common solutions to problems. This process of organizational fractionation has often been the consequence of Igbo individuals and groups attempting to gain leadership roles for themselves. Thus, there have been consistent failures in accomplishing large-group goals.

I believe that there has been an Igbo tendency to withdraw under the stress of conflict and to form their particular groupings. The formation of Biafra in 1967 was their major example of withdrawal although the reasons involved major losses of life, business, personal dwellings, and welfare in the north of Nigeria and the failure of the federal government to respond adequately to these issues. I see the Igbos' tendency to withdraw and reform under stress today, as generally undesirable in terms of the goals that the Igbos wish to achieve within Nigeria. It is another way of looking at the processes of organizational tendencies to divide and break up. This withdrawal quality may have had its roots in more traditional times when sections of a community broke away to form their group elsewhere within the same community, in a new community, or through joining another community. as a result of population increase, land shortages, or other factors. This tendency seems to continue today in modern Igboland.

Hegemony

Afikpo was a highly hegemonic society. Male dominance was everywhere. Girls married in adolescence to men aged twenty-five to eighty or so in arranged marriages where the future husband and parents of both parties had much more to say about the marriage arrangements than the girl. She was likely to have two or three consecutive husbands in her lifetime, living in different compounds of a village or in different villages. Early marriage maximized her baby-producing potential, which enhanced her husband's status, political position, and farming possibilities. Marriage was a social system that benefitted males at the expense of females.

Males controlled most spirit shrines, and females had to sacrifice at a number of these. The male village secret society was designed to control and to terrorize females. Women knew that the masqueraders were village men, but they feared the secret society spirit shrines associated with the masking.

Women were restricted to trading in villages a short distance from their own for fear of being kidnapped or due to the men's anxiety that their wives might be involved in sexual liaisons.

There were about twenty-five titled societies at Afikpo, ranked in status, of which women had only several titles. Title society membership was a major male preoccupation. At male title events, men enjoyed most of the palm wine and food while women did the cooking but received little food or drink. The higher the titles the male carried, the more considerable the prestige.

Religion

During the colonial period, the mainline Presbyterian, Methodist, and Anglican churches prospered in Igboland. Today their attendance is small. The Igbos have turned to smaller evangelical, fundamentalist, and charismatic religion groups. This allows for greater expression from the members of the religious orders.

Igbo National Unity

National Igbo coordination, from the 1950s and up to the beginning of the Biafran conflict in 1967, was largely through the nationalist political party, the National Council of Nigeria and the Cameroons (NCNC) under the leadership of the Igbo politician, Nnamdi Azikiwe, though his party also included members of other cultural groups. Between 1960 and throughout the Biafran war, the majority of the Igbos (excluding the Western

Igbo or Anioma) were under the Eastern Region, and there was some sense of unity in this dominant cultural group with numerous non-Igbo groups to the east and south also forming part of the region. During the Biafran conflict, there was a strong unity of Igbos, which, however, broke down as the conflict progressed and the Igbo front diminished. A consequence of the war was that the Igbos were placed in five states, Anambra, Abia, Imo and Enugu—with the Igbo in Aniona in the Delta State residing with other cultural groups, and in 1996, eastern and northeastern Igbo formed as Ebonyi State. This postwar state formation occurred and has continued to do so all over Nigeria under federal leadership. The consequence for the Igbos is that now their states compete with one another for federal resources, making pan-Igbo unity difficult despite recent motions toward regional autonomy for either the Igbos alone or for southeastern Nigeria, and there are talks of recreating a Biafran state. The problem with Igbo unity is not only the social and cultural style of its members as discussed above, making it difficult to agree to have a pan-Igbo policy, it is also clearly a product of external

Nigerian influences. The possibility of pan Igbo unity does not exist unless its areas come under a very extreme crisis.

Christianity

In the face of their achievement orientation and their external social, cultural, and political interests, the Igbos often have abandoned Igbo culture and religion for a variety of forms of Christianity. During colonialism, which ended in 1960, there were the "old-line" mission churches: Anglican, Catholic, Methodist, and Presbyterian, all of which made some pragmatic accommodations to Igbo traditions and still do today to some extent. But more recently, sometimes large, but often small, evangelical and apostolic churches have risen in Igboland. Here individuals of both genders have taken leadership roles in religious development where there are benefits for the church leaders as well as for its followers. These newer religions have risen all over southern Nigeria (and in many other parts of Africa) in the context of years of political and economic stress, anxiety, and considerable poverty, in which traditional cultural and ritual solutions to problems appear valueless. The existence of small Igbo Christian religious groups of the newer kind among the Igbos may be seen as another example of a withdrawal from larger organizations (the old-line churches) and an aspect of individuals striving for religious leadership roles. These enthusiastic religious organizations become spiritual families for individuals in the face of serious problems of disorganization and anomie in the country.

Some new Christian groups are strident, highly conforming, and mirror images of fundamentalist Islamic religious groups arising in Muslim areas of the country's north and elsewhere. In the Igbo case, due to the continuing intermittent killings and pogrom-like activities against them in the north, going back more than forty years, the development of strong Christian groups in Igboland is likely to be partly an unconscious, or conscious, defense of individual Igbos against Islam, a reaction to it. If the north will be Islamic, then the Igbo country will be Christian.

The Igbo experience with Christianity stands side by side with a great deal of corruption in Igboland, a good deal of which is carried out by those who claim to be Christian, either of old-line or new-line Christianity despite religious beliefs and moral rules, which suggest that such activities are abominations. Christian beliefs exist in an atmosphere where there is substantial egoistic and selfish political leadership detrimental to the best needs of society, again contradictory to church beliefs. These features, of course, are not unique to the Igbos but occur throughout Nigeria: they are endemic in the country, suggesting the extent of contradictions between Christian beliefs and everyday practice.

The Igbos' achievement orientation, and the Nigerian postcolonial conditions, including the Biafran War, have led the Igbos to abandon to a large extent many traditional customs, except the nostalgic and symbolic matter, something I find to be less true for southwestern Nigeria's Yoruba people. Igbo tradition is now basically Christian tradition, one now often officially supported by the government and by political officials. Jesus Christ and the Bible have become paramount in religious terms whether the associated rituals are in Igbo or English. Igbo traditional spirits, such as *ala*, the earth spirit of growth and welfare, and the ancestors as spirits, have largely lost their place in Igbo life, and many traditional Igbo shrines have disappeared along with their associated beliefs and practices. Igbo Christianity may differ to some extent from other Christian traditions in Nigeria, but Igbo indigenous culture is largely minimized within it. Some newer Christian fundamentalist groups are quite hostile to tradition, considering all its forms to be sinful They do much to stamp it out, more so than the old-line missionary groups ever did as if the root of Igbo problems today lay in tradition rather than elsewhere. This is a matter of misplaced concreteness. Many of these newer groups have connections to similar religious groups elsewhere in the world, particularly in the United States, some of which support them financially and spiritually and with personnel. In any case, Igbo tradition, which was localized largely to Nigeria and survived among some Igbo slave groups in America, has now largely been replaced by worldwide religious traditions. The globalization of Christianity in Igboland, which began during colonialism with the mission churches, is now very far along. European missionaries planted the seeds of Christianity, and Nigerians have taken it over, sometimes with surprising enthusiasm. It is now Igbo who are destroying Igbo tradition, not the expatriates.

Corruption

Corruption in Igboland, like elsewhere in Africa, may have had its roots in tradition, where it was not considered corruption at all, in that it was common practice to provide leaders, particularly elders, with gifts—generally but not always small—to ask them to discuss serious matters, to arbitrate disputes, and to adjudicate legal issues. Transferred to the modern Nigerian world, this opened up greater possibilities during colonialism and even more major ones since then, and while in the past, gifting was generally open, it has become secretive and does not necessarily just involve elders and leaders. Corruption is now a deeply held social tradition in Igboland and Nigeria regardless of religious belief. The advent of almost total Christianity in Igboland has not forestalled it. Since the government and the courts engage in it, there is no check on it, no balance. The Igbos are no more or less involved in it than others in the country.

Igbo Language and Tradition

The Igbo language survives and is healthy although the Igbo dialects are being supplemented by a pan-Igbo tongue while some Igbo families away from Igboland—in Nigeria, Europe, and America—do not teach their children the Igbo tongue. Nor do some parents living in Nigerian urban areas encourage their children and grandchildren to learn Igbo. The survival of this language may appear paradoxical since the older Igbo culture has mostly disappeared, yet the Igbo language has become the language of modernity and the church rather than the tongue of tradition. The words of tradition still exist in the Igbo language, but they are less employed than Igbo terms in modern life.

The Igbos still retain strong home communal ties and regional identity even when away from home. The social ties of birth, upbringing, descent, and respect of elders and ancestors continue to exist even if they are no longer viewed as spiritual forces that can assist or harm living individuals but as markers of kinship. Ancestral identity is not so much tied to indigenous religious tradition as to memories of past traditions and to common birth, residence, and language. The importance of the links to home through landholdings continues although the land is more and more becoming individually owned rather than communally held. The speaking of individual Igbos with other Igbos is still major, encouraged by their experiences in the past and present Nigeria. Social, professional, educational, business, and political matters evolved in Igboland, and Christianity has come to dominate tradition. Yet, being Igbo, and maintaning links to ancestral identities, remains strong even though many traditional cultural attributes have disappeared.

There are still elements of tradition in Igboland: kola rituals, marriage rites, some masquerades, and some titling, though now many Igbo prefer to put their funds into education and business. There is much emphasis on the installation of chiefs at every locale when they did not exist in precolonial times. Expansive and expensive memorial services for the dead are now popular, blending Igbo tradition and Christianity, and for which, the Igbos return home. Initiation rites still occur in some instances, but much of their symbolism has been lost, and they are quite foreshortened in time due to the practical restraints of those being initiated and their families. Female singing and dancing groups exist with modified traditional elements, appearing on ceremonial occasions, and so-called *uli* creators in the art program at the University of Nigeria, Nsukka, draw from tradition for design and images. A number of local Igbo communities have members who have written community histories or biographies about their prominent citizens; these often include cultural information on traditions and are often publications that express communal Igbo history, tradition, and religion written by professionally trained Igbo scholars, mostly by authors no longer living these traditions, some of whom no longer reside in Igbo country. There have been prominent Igbo historians who, necessarily, deal with traditional cultural materials, such as the late Don Ohadike, the still-practicing Adele Amigo, and Ogbu O. Kalu. But the overall picture is one of putting aside and actually losing a sense of identity and empathy with the past. There is nostalgia for it, but not enough to keep it going. This is the paradox: Igbo social and ethnic identity survives, but Igbo tradition is dying out.

The Igbo War and the Possibilities of Igbo Revival

The Biafran War did much to end indigenous belief and practice; for, during the war, traditional shrines and ritual objects were destroyed, ritual groups dispersed, or its members died or were killed, and hunger and poverty made the carrying out of tradition difficult while, at the same time, it bonded the Igbos close to each other in ethnic identity. After the conflict, there were recoveries by rebuilding shrines, redeveloping rituals and masquerades, and recreating traditional age grades, men's and women's societies, and so on, but the tradition was never quite the same. Understandably so. For some Igbos, the failure to win the war was linked in their minds to the failure of tradition to fully support them in the conflict. The old gods and spirits did not help

Biafra gain victory. New religious ways were sought after its end, and Christianity came to play the explanatory role for success.

The slowly developing modernization of Igboland in the years immediately after the Biafran War moved individuals and groups away from tradition to other more attractive interests, whose process accelerated after the profound shocks of the conflict were eased with time. Business and professional concerns became and have remained paramount, and they do not generally favor Igbo tradition, another pulling away from it. Christianity contains values that favor commercialization, not only within the church but in the daily lives of its members. Business concerns and Christianity, acting side by side, have encouraged the demise of traditional practices.

The processes of moving away from tradition have not been gender specific: females, as well as males, have been involved. Women have been particularly active in the Christian churches, including the newer, more fundamentalist ones, both as members and as leaders. Women, as well as men, have been much involved in business, not surprising considering Igbo women's traditional trading and marketing roles. Often denied education during colonial times, as priorities went to males, women have strongly advanced in modern education at all levels. And they are the active in current politics. Women have played major roles in the demise of Igbo tradition, as have males, although both genders retain some indigenous Igbo family practices and usually the Igbo language..

These reflections on Igbo culture and society lead me to another point. And that is that the historical studies that Don Ohadike carried out on the Igbos are important treasures in the analysis of Igbo tradition, as has been the work of other historians of the Igbos and the scholars of its religion and culture. And surviving archival materials and photographs are valuable historical assets. The researches of both Nigerian and Western anthropologists have also contributed to the recording of Igbo culture. Not only are these important records of the past, but they are something that Igbos today can identify with and cherish, even if they no longer live these past traditions. The existence of written records on the Igbo, such as those of Don Ohadike, allow for the possibility of future ethnic revival of selective Igbo traditional elements, whether this idea seems far-fetched today or not. Without these documents, once the memory of past Igbo culture and society is gone, as senior Igbos pass away, this becomes impossible.

Ethnic revitalization has occurred among Native Americans (e.g., American Indians) when the loss of tradition was largely externally imposed by white Americans and Canadians, aided by some native peoples who saw no future at the time in following their own traditions. In the past thirty years, ethnic revivals among Native Americans (and First Nations Peoples, as indigenous Canadians call themselves) have not only made use of the memories of elders, but of published and unpublished materials by historians, anthropologists, government officials, and explorers and in museum collections. This has allowed many Native American communities to reconstruct aspects of their past traditions while adjusting to living in the modern world. They have reconstituted sacred religious elements, dances, initiations, music, art, myths, traditional buildings, ceremonies, and some everyday customs and beliefs. Native Americans are teaching their members their own languages to keep these alive and to use these on special occasions, and they are developing what are, for them, new art forms, such as working with silkscreen, glass and silver, gold and iron, as well as reviving traditional carving and painting techniques. Such ethnic revivals have occurred among Australian Aborigines and other Third World peoples, and within the Second and First World. The popularity of multiculturalism in the West has encouraged various ethnic revivals there. The cultures in the world have gone through periods of revival where drawing from the past becomes important to the present. The Serbs, for better or worse, are an example, not to speak of the Croats and the Montenegrins. At one time in European history Europeans forgot the impact of ancient Greece and Rome on their lives and cultures. They again became aware of these, and this influenced European architecture, art, literature and customs, and perhaps, politics. Of course, an ethnic revival never means a total return to tradition, but only the selection of aspects of it in modified form, elements that mesh with whatever exists. And it can only occur under certain conditions.

I would not argue that an Igbo ethnic revival based on past

traditions is likely to occur in the immediate future. The depth of the influence of Christianity and modern life precludes it. But the potential exists for it to occur. If an Igbo ethnic revival based on past traditions ever arises, it will occur under conditions of powerful negative political and economic pressures from the outside, through a growing disillusionment with modernity in Nigeria, or both. Then the published and archival records of scholars, such as those of Don Ohadike, would become extremely useful tools to help select what elements from the past would be of value. This is but one reason to treasure th Igbo's past. Even if there is never an ethnic revival that draws upon older traditions, Igbo research and writings instruct us as to how the Igbos lived and behaved in the past, sometimes under duress; they serve as social models for tomorrow.

Dibia

A doctor or medicine man; one who prepares curative (or poisonous) medicines; diviner; spiritualist; one who can intercede (through divination or sacrifices) with the spirit world on behalf of clients; fortune-teller (from Michael J. C. Echeruo, *Igbo English Dictionary* [New Haven: Yale University Press, 1998], 38). *Dibias* formerly existed in numerous villages or groups of villages in Igboland in southeastern Nigeria. There must have been 250 *dibias* in all, given the high population numbers and widespread nature of Igbo population. They were quite independent of one another, acting alone within a large Igbo population, except that a dibia was usually trained by another dibia. They were popular, well-attended, and generally considered to be very helpful in resolving personal and interpersonal disputes. Although mostly male, there were several well-known women dibias. It was often inherited from father to son, preferably the father's first son. It was sometimes taught to a nonrelative, particularly if such a person had a dream concerning dibias, though the holder of such a role usually was thought to have less prestige and influence than dibias who inherited the position.

To consult a dibia, one sometimes just would go to the diviner's hut, put down the money, and begin a discussion with a visible dibia. Other Igbo dibias had more complicated procedures. The client would bring the fee and sit in front of the dibia's hut, which was barred by a closed wooden door. The dibia would make strange wailing and other sounds and then ask the client a question (for example, "You are having a problem with your lineage") or he might suggest something to the client's family, or something else. If the answer to any of that was a no from the client, the dibia would continue producing mysterious hidden sounds related to his spirit world. The client would continue to say no to the dibia's queries until the client named the correct person, group, or situation. Then there would be a silence from the dibia, as a hand would reach out from the back of the screen and gather up the fee, usually in coins. This was followed by a period of further strange sounds as the dibia consulted his spirits. Then a voice would suggest a solution to the client's problem, which the client generally accepted as it came from the spiritual world.

Dibias lived openly in villages, freely interacting with its members, and they often had a good ear for gossip, so they usually did not take long to detect the client's problem, given his or her age and gender.

Once trained as a dibia, the person held that position for life. The dibia could see through the wooden screen but could not be seen by the client as his hut was dark, and of course, the client did not view any objects that the dibia manipulated to create spiritual sounds.

The dibia's recommendation often was of a sacrifice to one or more village shrines or at a neighborhood shrine, the wearing of a protective charm of stone or wood for a period of time, or a visit to a more specialized dibia at some distance from the village. Dibias were believed to be capable of poisoning someone for a client's fee, making him ill. Or this was used as an explanation for a death shortly after visiting a dibia. The spiritualist was carefully treated in the village where he lived, generally where he was born, and villagers stayed away and avoided conflict with him.

<u>Dibias</u> often avoided leadership roles in the social and political aspects of village life although they may have married one or more females living in the village. In a few instances, there was a group of dibias from neighboring areas who had a social group that might set the working rules for its members. But in most cases, dibias set their own standards based on training and work experience. There was certainly a great deal of variation in the style and interests of the various dibias.

Many deaths of people or animals in a village brought in a dibia. Before the start of the planting season, issues as to who would plant where had to be resolved. Occasionally, there would be conflicts over this that neither the lineage nor lineages involved were able to resolve. If the village leaders could not, a dibia might be called to settle the matter, and this usually was the case. If a party to the land-use dispute was still not satisfied, the issue would go to a special shrine for one of the parties to the dispute, often chosen by the village leaders, to swear the correctness of his or her case. If that person became ill or died within a year, it was clear where the guilt lay.

At the request of the village elders, usually the community leaders, a dibia might bless the planting of the new rice, yam, or other crops regardless of where the crop, or crops, was located. An object believed to have magical power, such as a piece of iron, an old dish, or a forked stake, might be placed on the crop to ensure good growth and to protect it from theft. If the crop was poor, the village dibia might be consulted as to the reason, and a few individuals in the village might question the <u>dibia's</u> ability. He, in turn, had an explanation for the crop's failure, which lay elsewhere from what he could control. If the crop was a success, the dibia might be praised by the village leaders.

A number of dibias were also farmers or fishermen, as the work of the dibia, particularly in the smaller Igbo communities, was not full-time.

A dibia could be involved in a wide range of activities. There seemed to be no limits to what he might be concerned with. He was frequently involved in an individual's illness or, when an individual had an accident, attempting to discover who was poisoning or affecting the patient. In such cases, the dibia might indicate that a spirit was involved, as well as another individual, and he would suggest how to cope with this problem. In such cases, the dibia, either directly or indirectly, might indicate the person or persons involved. A dibia might provide the cause of death, and if a spirit was implicated in the death, the dibia could resolve the matter, leading to decreased tension among the parties involved, or it could lead to increased antagonism. From the dibia's viewpoint, he was only doing what his spirits directed him to do. Yet he must have known that a solution in a dispute, or case, brought either resolution or more conflict, at least by one of the parties involved.

Disputes over personal property, particularly over the ownership of a gun when its owner died, might lead to a dibia for resolution, for guns were of value to hunters in obtaining meat for sale.

Before a wrestling match, a contestant might obtain a charm from a dibia and hide it in his waistcloth when he competed to bring himself the victory.

A client of a dibia in his village was free to consult a second dibia in another village if he was not satisfied with his village dibia's decision in a matter. The idea was that an external dibia would not be influenced by local issues and could provide a clearer view of the problem involved. The local village dibia was too close to his village's social life and politics to make a fair judgment. Or some dibia's clients thought that if their village dibia did not come to the conclusions that the client wanted, then the ultimate end of this approach would be a consultation with the Igbo oracle located in a different section of Igboland. It would be an expensive endeavor. This procedure would likely be used in farmland ownership disputes, personal property disputes, or cases of murder charges.

Consulting a dibia was common before undertaking a long trip or any major endeavor. Popular consultation with a dibia end was in making a long trip, or before taking a major title, which brought honor and prestige to its owner, although a dibia's recommendations did not always ensure the success of the title taking. At the minimum, it assured the positive backing of major spiritual forces in the title-taker's mind. Occasionally, the dibia would recommend a delay, as the spiritual time was not favorable to proceed, but the title taker might go ahead with the series of events and rituals associated with the title anyway. The fees for such a consultation to the dibia were higher than in many other dibia consultations.

A considerable amount of time and energy of the dibia's was spent on human health issues in a culture lacking in modern medicine. If someone felt ill, and even the concept of "feeling ill" was culturally determined, one had several choices. One could do nothing and hope that it went away. One could recognize it as a feeling one had before and treat it as before. One could consult friends or a relative. One could consult a herbalist, or one could consult a dibia. If the condition persisted over a long period of time, one could visit an Igbo oracle. Many cases of illness were considered to be the result of someone working magic or witchcraft on a person. The suspected witch was often living with or close to the victim and not far away. Belief in witchcraft was endemic. One way of driving away a witch was through a dibia, but there were many other ways. A dibia might point to a specific individual or just make a suggestion as to the cause. The dibia was a central figure in Afikpo culture, usually a quiet individual who worked privately and in mysterious ways.

Gabriel Anigo Agwo
Book Review

Gabriel Anigo Agwo, A Diary of *My Journey Through Life* (Lagos: Mbeyi and Associate,), 422 pages.

The autobiography of an Igbo from Amaizu in Afikpo, southeastern Nigeria. He was born in about 1933. In writing this memoir, Gabriel made use of his mother's knowledge of his childhood, and as an adult, he has kept records of his life until the time of publication, except those lost during the Biafran War in 1967–1970. He is educated, having lived a modem life in Nigeria, and is a Catholic. He also has been devoted to Igbo tradition, knows it well, and has published a number of articles on it on the web and in the journal, *Afikpo Today*. He prefers the more phonetically accurate term Ehugbo to Afikpo. He has visited the United States and Kenya. At Afikpo, he holds the title of Horii, indicating that he is of the most senior and honorable age.

His parents were born in the same village although in different sections. Gabriel had several siblings who lived to adulthood, others died at birth or when they were young. His father, who had five wives, in middle age left for Calabar and worked there and elsewhere on the coast and the Cross River for a few years. He was considered to be a rich man, but no fortune was found for his family when he died at forty-five years of age, and it may have been stolen.

His mother was able to earn enough money (probably through trading some of what she grew and sold at Afikpo markets) to put Gabriel through the local Afikpo government primary school between 1950 and 1958 despite some illness on his part. He passed the Standard VI Examination in 1948, but he failed to obtain admission to a college in Lagos where he had applied. He became interested in Catholicism, and in that year, he was baptized and given the name of Gabriel.

Following a year of trading with a friend on the Cross River from Afikpo to Ikom to Calabar and back to Afikpo, he spent a year in preparatory school. He was then assigned to St Mary's

School at Afikpo where he developed his teaching skills between 1951 and 1957, which he details at length. He passed the next level of government tests for teachers, and he taught at the Elementary Teachers' College at Obudu, away from Afikpo country. Then, eventually, he returned to St. Mary's to teach, and then to Izzi in Abakaliki, where he was when the Biafran War broke out in 1957.

Gabriel describes the bombing of Afikpo by federal aircraft and the early fall of Afikpo to federal troops, his capture with others, and how a few of them escaped. He discusses his life as a refugee during the war but not as a soldier. The war ended with the defeat of Biafra in early 1960. Gabriel and his family returned home to rebuild their lives, and he had again a brief period of teaching in Abakaliki.

He studied French in secondary school, and he was admitted to the University of Nigeria at Nsukka, in southeastern Nigeria, into the French program, which he did not want. However, he completed the course and then continued a program in education and general studies in English. He was at the university from 1974 to 1977.

He then again taught at Izzi in Abakaliki, and he developed a series of plans. One was to rebuild his compound, but others living there did not always cooperate, and the plan lagged. Another project was the rebuilding of his own home.

He was committed to reviving the Afikpo Town Welfare Association. This organization was started during the end of the colonial period. By then, there were very few Western-educated individuals at Afikpo to uplift it by doing improvements at home. It was largely dependent on the branches of ATWA in the cities, where salaried Afikpo workers were living and could help finance projects in Afikpo Town, such as an improved quality of the water supply and school scholarships. Gabriel helped to revive ATWA, but he apparently did not hold office in it.

Gabriel was also involved in an attempt to appoint a well known traditional elder to be the honorary head for an Igbo region that was larger than Afikpo but included it. But there was a continual dispute as to who had the right to hold this position. On one side, there were the Amadi, or people from a southern Igbo group of the Arochukwu who were living in

Afikpo and formerly dealt in slavery, or their ancestors did. They possessed a powerful shrine that some Afikpo had purchased, and thus, they became Amadi. These Igbo claimed that they had the political right to appoint this figure. On the other side, a much larger group of freeborn Igbo claimed that the Amadi were interlopers and had no right to make the appointment, a position that Gabriel advocated. The dispute went on endlessly without resolution.

Gabriel attended a two-week Catholic conference in Nairobi. He helped to ensure that the new Akanu Ibiam Federal Polytechnic would be placed in Afikpo. He was involved in the growth of the Afikpo Technical College At one time, he served as the principal of Nzuzu Edda Community Secondary School, Edda being a neighboring Igbo ethnic group. That same year, he was made a senior supervisor of schools at Afikpo, his final public service position, in which role he facilitated the establishment of the Ozizza Comprehensive School in Afikpo.

He describes his continued activities, both public and private, until the end of the book.

Gabriel contributed considerably to the growth of Afikpo and the surrounding area, particularly in the educational field, despite the problems resulting from the Biafran War. He did not move to a Nigerian city or Britain or to the United States, during or as a consequence of the conflict like a considerable number of Igbo did, but he remained centered in the Afikpo region. He helped to restore it after the conflict and went on to make a remarkably successful career, sometimes negotiating with federal or regional governments. He published accounts over the years about Afikpo's Igbo traditions. He has not forgotten or suppressed the past, as a considerable number of Igbo have. He did personally put a good deal of it aside after the war, but he has not renounced its importance in the history of Igbo life.

From Anthropology to Contemporary Art

Simon Ottenberg

In 1992–1993, I moved from my usual base in Seattle, where I was writing my research in West African anthropology, to Washington DC, to become involved as the curator of an exhibition of what is now called contemporary art. I had called it modern art at the time, naively unaware that modern art in art history referred to art in Europe from the 1860s to the 1970s when there was a radical movement in art, for I was ignorant of art history. However, the art in Nigeria that I was interested in is post-1879 and is called contemporary art. I now use the proper term, contemporary. I had authored some articles on individual contemporary Nigerian artists, and I was intrigued by them, as I had written about traditional artists. But I had never been a curator of a major museum exhibition before. It took time and considerable assistance from the curators and the staff for me to figure out what my roles were in the exhibition.

It was Roy Sieber at Indiana University, the leading academic in the training of scholars interested in the study of traditional African arts, who, in 1991, suggested that should I apply for a year's fellowship at the National Museum of African Art in Washington DC to do anything I wished. This worked out for the 1992–1993 academic yea

I thought about research in Zambia, but there I would have to start with no background. During the year I went to the University of Nigeria, Nsukka, the leading university in Nigeria's southeast, and received an Honorary D. Literature for my anthropological research over the years on the Igbos, the major ethnic group in southeastern Nigeria. After the ceremony, I was introduced to a leading contemporary artist at the university, Obiora Udechukwu, who invited me to the annual meeting and exhibition the next day of AKA Circle of Exhibiting Artists, which had begun in 1986 and included many of the contemporary artists in Nigeria's southeast. This gathering turned out to be a fascinating small group of diverse contemporary artists, varied in techniques, media, and content. Most of them had trained at, or were influenced by, the University of Nigeria, Nsukka's Art Department head, Uche Okeke, who drew his designs from traditional Igbo women's designs in black or blue, on their head and arms, legs, and the body, painted on themselves or on one another and on house and compound walls. These were known as *uli*, which were purely decorative. But some AKA artists, many students of Okeke, and other local contemporary artists were combining uli with political statements concerning the neglect of southeastern Nigeria's Christian population by Nigeria's Muslim northern leaders.

I came back to America convinced that an exhibition of the work of some of these artists associated with, or influenced by, the art department at the University of Nigeria, Nsukka, would work although I realized that I had never curated a major exhibit and would have to rely on the curatorial judgments more than I cared for. From my photographs, field notes, collected catalogs and other publications, and other sources, the curators and I spent hours choosing seven artists.

I returned to Nigeria and interviewed each one intensely. I came back home thinking about what my major contribution to the future exhibition *would be like*.

The background to the exhibition was after Nigerian independence in 1960, most of the Christian Igbos in the southeast increasingly felt that they were neglected by the Muslim northerners who dominated Nigeria and showed little interest in the southeast. Okeke, who was familiar with uli designs from his home area, merged uli with images of Nigerian leaders' incompetency, corruption, and selfishness, incorporating these elements into the same work, and merging traditional Igbo body designs with contemporary political issues. This style of art became popular with his students and spread beyond the classroom. The Igbos' complaints appeared in the art form to complement those voiced and written criticism of the federal government.

The question as to why the Nsukka program turned to politics is best understood when related to the Igbo failure to succeed Nigeria in the 1967–1970 Biafran War with Nigeria, which reaffirmed in many Igbos who survived the war the continuous sense of false leadership in Nigeria. It made sense that the artists would be antagonistic to the Nigerian government and depict, sometimes in almost cartoon style, the many appalling government actions, its corruption, and its deceit.

It was the first and only major exhibition that I ever curated. I have had some years as an anthropologist, researching Igbo culture, and felt confident that this would be of use. In Nigeria, I gathered data in an anthropological fashion on the artists and photographs of them and their art for the curators.

Fifty artworks were shipped from Nigeria in good condition. Their placement on the museum walls by artist rather than by content was the museum curator's decision, simplifying matters. I would have preferred to locate the art by content, but the curators argued that this would be confusing to the public. A 302-page catalog of the exposition was published during the exhibition although my copy is dated 1997.

Six of the seven artists and African art scholars came to the museum during the exhibition and held a lively two-day seminar leading to the publication of the proceeding in 330 pages (Ottenberg 2002).

The museum went all out in this first major contemporary African art show as if to announce that they were now fully committed to contemporary African art. And they were as further exhibitions on the subject would appear to balance their continuing interest in the older African arts.

For me, the exposition was a success. Enough was enough for me. I could have gone into the history and origin of uli, its patterns, and into further reasons why Okeke chose to focus on uli and politics, and that he was creating in these two styles before he became the head of the art school. And to place the exhibition in the context of other early anthropology and contemporary art exhibitions elsewhere in Africa and the world and try to explain the marked differences in style of the seven chosen artists would have enriched an already full account of the seven artists too greatly.

This exhibition was an early one in the yet-to-be-developed field of anthropology and contemporary art. It was only preceded by a small but thoughtful exhibition on African art at the Harlem Studio Museum. And by two others at this museum. I might have benefitted from the later theoretical work, but it succeeded in its aims. Today, this field is known as anthropology and contemporary art, which now has its journal (*Field*), researchers, and theorists (see references). I would undoubtedly have benefited from their existence, but I felt that we did a capable job.

References

"AKA: Circle of Exhibiting Artists 1986." (Enugu, Nigeria, Annual Exhibition).

Banks, Markus and Howard Morphy, eds. *Rethinking Visual Anthropology*. 1999. Yale University Press.

Field: A Journal of Socially Engaged Art Criticism. 2015. Fillitz, Thomas and Paul van der Grijp. 2018. *An Anthropology of Contemporary Art*. London: Bloomsbury.

Gell, Alfred. 1998. *Art and Agency: An Anthropological Theory*. Oxford: Oxford University Press.

Marcus, George E. and Fred R. Myers, eds. 1995. *The Traffic in Culture: Refiguring Art and Anthropology*. Berkeley: University of California Press.

Ottenberg, Simon. 1997. *New Traditions from Nigeria: Seven Artists of the Nsukka Group*. Washington DC: Smithsonian Institution Press.

Ottenberg, Simon, ed. 2002. *The Nsukka Artists and Nigerian Contemporary Art.* Washington DC: Smithsonian Institution Press.

Schneider, Adam and Wright, Christopher, eds. *Between Art and Anthropology: Ethnographic Practice.* New York: Berg. Svasek, Marusk. 2007. *Anthropology, Art and Cultural Production.* London: Pluto Press.

Tyler, Stephen A. 1987. *The Unspeakable Discourse: Dialog and Rhetoric in the Postmodern World.* Madison: University of Wisconsin Press.

Selections from an Interview with Simon Ottenberg

by GR, an anonymous female reporter for the journal

Glendora Review in 1993. Interview at the National

Museum of African Art, Smithsonian Institution,

Washington DC with additional comments.

GR. Art historians learn the details of surface qualities and the knowledge of styles and style language whereas anthropologists have little awareness, nor how a work is constructed, and little awareness of how it is created, unless he observes this. The art historian is better at understanding the color choices and the art techniques.

While a few anthropologists have successfully described contemporary art, there is not a large number in this group. Recently, perhaps in defense of the need for scholarly work and identity and an unwillingness to see the anthropology of art becoming primarily the study of museum collections, anthropology has redefined itself into the anthropology of contemporary art (see references above). This approach opens up endless tasks for the anthropologist.

I had the feeling that the museum/art history approach dominated my work on the exhibit, but now I don't think it is so. Every piece I chose for the exhibit was accepted. I wrote the captions. They were too long, I was told, for captions. People could read the catalog. I took field photographs of the art, and the museum took out a lot more. I was interviewed by the press. The museum worked out the flow of the exhibit. I was involved in the editing of the accompanying papers; presented at a two-day symposium which I coedited. It was published by the Smithsonian Institution press. I never learned where the money came from. I have always thought it came from the museum.

That the exhibition went very well without all the later scholarly development of theories in anthropology and contemporary art is interesting. I am not sure that theory would have enhanced it significantly.

Interview

GR: How does your experience as an anthropologist differ from your current work in art history?

Ottenberg: Well, I may be turning into a pseudo-art historian who is trying to learn about style and technique and so on. When I was an anthropologist in Afikpo in the 1950s and early '60s, most of the people I was working with were not literate. It was a very traditional society, and I knew I was writing more or less for a Western audience. I thought my writings would only be read by people here, but over the years, this has turned out to be very incorrect because the literacy level went up and individuals have read my books and articles at the University of Nigeria and other places. There was a sense of greater distance between my subject and my subjects. Here I am trying to do a study of Nsukka artists, a highly literate group who themselves wrote a great deal, including poetry. They also can offer criticism of any article I write, such as my paper at the Second International Symposium on Contemporary Nigerian Act in Lagos in 1993. The dialogue is very different. Most of it is in English while before most of the dialogue was either in Igbo or pidgin English, and that makes for a different experience. I was never trained in European art, and I was never trained in aesthetics. I think I have a pretty good eye for traditional art, but I am trying to retrain myself to get an understanding of how to see contemporary art. I don't always succeed. I remember looking at a watercolor by Tayo Adenaike. After a long time observing the painting, I could not help but ask what it was about. He said it is the face of a man with his glasses on. As soon as he said that I saw it. In a sense, I am still learning to see. That is a handicap. The strength that I may be bringing to my work with Nsukka artists is knowledge of traditional Igbo culture.

GR: How did you become interested in Afikpo as an anthropologist?

Ottenberg: I saw myself as a rebellious student, as did my wife, Phoebe. At that time, we were students at Northwestern University, studying anthropology with a man who started the first major African studies program in the United States, Professor Melville J. Herskovits, who did research in Dahomey. There was also William Bascom, who was a well-known Yoruba scholar who worked in Ife on Ifa divination. Phoebe and I decided that since Herskovits had done his studies in the early 1930s, we would do a restudy in Dahomey. But Professor Herskovits did not think that was a good idea. He was wise. Because he was very much involved in that study, it would have been difficult to write anything that might be critical of his Dahomey research.

William Bascom suggested we should work on the Ibo, now written and pronounced Igbo by scholars and others. He had not researched this very large population group in southeastern Nigeria. However, he had once visited an Igbo village and obtained a significant number of its attractive masks, some of which we had seen at his home. We decided to work in an Igbo area that had never been studied before. We chose the Ohafia region, and we were in a nearby colonial office in Nigeria in December 1951. However, the provincial officer and the district officer for the Ohafia area politely told us we could not go to Ohafia because of land wars and bad roads, and the area was isolated. We then wired the district officer in Afikpo, J. D. Livingston-Booth, who had studied a little anthropology in Cambridge in a postgraduate colonial service course. Afikpo was in the northern section of the same Igbo subculture as Ohafia although in a different Nigerian province. The district officer telegraphed us that he would be glad to have us. He found us a place to live at Afikpo and helped us to find field assistants, as there had been no Igbos available in the United [States] to teach us the Igbo language.

GR: At what point did you decide to go into contemporary Nigerian art, considering the fact that you have had a very successful and distinguished career as an anthropologist?

Ottenberg: I must tell you first that at Northwestern, Herskovits and Bascom were very much interested in traditional African art, and I had an interest too. In 1975, I published a book on the Afikpo masquerades and some related articles after that. My interest in contemporary art goes back to 1952 when I bought two little watercolors by Akinfe Okiki, who was painting in the dominant style of the period. Then in the early 1960s, in Lagos,

I bought several paintings by Osogbo. When I came to Lagos in 1966, [I] bought some art from the Gong Gallery, and from the Bronze Gallery..

GR: But how and why did you decide to begin serious research in contemporary Nigerian art?

Ottenberg: In 1990, Roy Sieber, the doyen of African art history at Indiana University, called me up from the National Museum of African Art in Washington DC. He wanted to know if I was interested in a one-year fellowship at the Smithsonian Institution. I was retiring from the University of Washington, so it did not seem like a bad idea. He suggested I should consider research on an aspect of contemporary African art. I was overwhelmed and incredibly surprised because I didn't realize that Roy was interested in contemporary African art although the Museum of African [Art] had had one exhibit of Sokari Douglas-Camp and one other very small exhibit. I thought about the prospect, and then I sent in a very general proposal. Roy didn't like some of the authors I cited because he didn't like their work, but it went through, and I was lucky to get what is referred to as a Regent

Fellowship, which was an all-Smithsonian Fellowship. It was not given by any specific Smithsonian Museum. Everything was set, but I hadn't decided on where I wanted to work since I did not commit myself to any particular area in the proposal. I came to Nsukka to receive an honorary degree, doctor of letters, in 1992. After the official ceremonies, there was a private party in my honor, and it was there that I met a major contemporary artist, Obiora Udechukwu. I told him about my interests in modern art, and he invited me to a meeting of the AKA Circle of Artists the very next day. The meeting was at Nsikak's house, and most of the members were in attendance. After our initial discussions, I thought that this was what I was looking for. I later talked with Udechukwu a bit, suggesting to him the possibility of drawing from the things I already knew rather than going to another part of Africa where I would be starting out afresh.

GR: So you thought there was some kind of familiarity with your Afikpo experience, considering that this too was somewhere east of the Niger?

Ottenberg: I felt very much at home, and I still do.

GR: Do you then think that your earlier work on Afikpo influenced your interest in the Nsukka/Enugu artists while the coincidence of meeting Udechukwu or even you coming to Nsukka for the honorary degree were a catalyst that heightened the deep interest in the area? You still could have done your research elsewhere in Africa in spite of the initial contacts with the AKA Circle.

Ottenberg: I was thinking of Zambia as one of the areas I could do my research. One of my former students, Karen Tranberg Hansen, who has been working in urban Zambia for years, had given me the names of some artists and some catalogs. I thought Zambia was a possibility too, but maybe I just got lazy. Maybe I decided on an area where I had some background information and where I knew the country well although I wasn't as intensely familiar with the Anambra State as I am now. It made sense, and when I came back to Igboland the next fall, receiving a chieftaincy title from Afikpo, I spent time at Nsukka where I started to talk to artists there. Then I came in the spring of 1993 for the international symposium in Lagos, and in 1994, I returned to Lagos. The project continued to develop, and I am very content. I have had wonderful cooperation from everybody in terms of the willingness of the artists who show their art, photographs, catalogs, and their Xeroxed materials. It was just wonderful.

GR: How similar is the research methodology of anthropology and that of art history from your experience?

Ottenberg: They are basically the same in the way I take notes and conduct interviews. The subject is different but granted that I don't need interpreters now, I still have to take notes. What is different is the voluminous number of publications available, including some very fine theses by students of the University of Nigeria, Nsukka. Now there is a lot more literature to cover. I am doing more history this time although when I worked at Afikpo, I had tried to trace things, such as the very complicated kinship system and the matrilineal, as well as patrilineal, groupings. I tried to trace where some of the masquerades came from, but I was basically doing a study at one point in time. Here I feel you have to go back to Uche Okeke and the Zaria group of artists. In fact, I have to go back to the beginning of contemporary art in Nigeria. I am planning to write a largely historical account that may be divided into periods in which the Nsukka artists have gone through certain growth and changes. These changes will be put into the given social contexts. What did the artists do during the Biafran War of 1967–1970? What effect did the war have on their art before and after cessation of hostilities? Another important social landmark is the oil boom, and one would want to find out its effect on Nsukka artists, and to a large extent, Nigeria.

GR: Have you seen what artists are producing elsewhere beyond the Nsukka-Enugu axis?

Ottenberg: I have not done too much of that. What I have been basically doing is whenever I come to Nigeria, I try to spend some time in Lagos. For instance, after the international symposium, I spent over a week there, and during that time, I saw the Uche Okeke and Obiora Udechukwu retrospectives, and I also saw an Ife Art School exhibit and a number of other shows. I later went up to Ife. I have not been elsewhere in the country other than Enugu, where I have talked to a number of artists, some of whom trained at Nsukka while others didn't share an interest in uli designs and other Igbo designs. And then I have been reading art catalogs and articles on art in other areas. I have some familiarity with Osogbo art because I have collected it. Nike Davies comes to the United States, and I have bought her art. I have a few early Twins Seven-Seven works, and I have also talked to artists at the Yaba College of Technology.

GR: Let us talk about Osogbo. You said you collected some art from there in the early 1960s?

Ottenberg: Yes. For example, Ogundele art and several Afolabi pieces and a couple of early Twins Seven-Seven works before he even started numbering his prints.

GR: At the time you collected those prints, what was your interest? For what reasons did you collect them?

Ottenberg: Well, I thought they were exciting. I didn't know what to do with them. As an anthropologist, I was simply aware there was something new going on, and it was visually attractive and suggested to me that creativity was taking some new forms. You have to know that I am a collector too. I am a possessive person about material things. I have many African masks. I have collected American Indian art from around the Seattle area where I live, but that is more recent. The year my wife and I were in Ghana, 1970–71, there was one contemporary gallery in Accra where I bought art.

I think there is a kind of curiosity coupled with the fact that my wife and I have no children, so we have a little more to put into art. The 1960s, I think, was the best period for Osogbo art. Much art degenerated afterward. I saw an exhibit last November at the National Museum, Lagos, that was absolutely awful. The basis for any discussion of contemporary Nigerian art, one begins to wonder whether it is because of the element of the quaint, the exotic that captures the interest of Western scholarship and patronage.

Much of Osogbo art has a fantasy quality to it and also has, I have to use the word because I am an anthropologist, a kind of primitivistic quality that fits into Western conceptions of what African art should be. This kind of art is attractive. There is a Ghanaian artist who does decorative coffins in the shape of a

Mercedes or an airplane. Americans go gaga about him. The Africa Explores exhibit showed this art. They are a kind of kitsch art, which is attractive and fits Western conceptions of what art should be like.

GR: Is it what art should be specifically for Africa or for the West and elsewhere?

Ottenberg: I don't object to Osogbo art. I am very ecumenical about art, much more so than most people, perhaps because I am not an artist. For example, there is a kind of genre of art in Nigeria which is sort of fairly naturalistic, fairly romanticized with beach scenes, durbars, drummers, masquerades, and all. A lot of it may not be technically superb, but it appeals to a certain group of people. There is an American artist, Norman Rockwell, who does that kind of art. He has been very popular, and he has done magazine covers for years. I call such art the Norman Rockwell art of Nigeria. It isn't great, but that does mean that you cannot do very fine scenes of a masquerade or durbar and so on, but much of this does not appeal to me. I can understand that it appeals to certain people, but with my own work, which will culminate in an exhibit of about seven of the Nsukka artists at the National Museum of African Art, Washington DC in 1997, I am hoping to bring a different view of one aspect of Nigerian art. GR: What's the aspect that appeals to you then?

Ottenberg: I like the Nsukka style very much. I like the emphasis on uli. I am fascinated by *nsibidi* and other design systems. I am fascinated by the process of drawing from traditional Igbo designs, yet making very modern statements about political and social conditions in this country. It is a beautiful blend. In a sense, the Nsukka group is not a kind of nostalgic group that is just looking at the past and romanticizing it and having some unconscious wish to return to the past as has occurred, for example, in early writing from South Africa, when writers wrote novels about Chaka Zulu and the rest. Those were great stories, but it was as if there were some attempts to return to the past. I think the artists in the Nsukka area are very realistic. They are very grounded in the present, and yet realistically, they are saying we have this heritage, and it's a rich one. Let's draw from it.

GR: Edwin Debebs and others have argued that the world is tending towards a global community, and as such, that art should be moving toward post modernist globalism. In this projected world art arena, any attempt by the African artist to draw from the past would be a kind of retrogressive atavism. Is there anything worthwhile about this nascent internationalism anyway?

Ottenberg: I was at a conference in April (1994) on New International Art at the Tate Gallery. Olu Oguibe was there, and he presented a paper. Bruce Onobrakpeya came from Nigeria. My impression from that conference is that the problems of artists living in Africa and those living in the West are somewhat different. There is a group of very fine artists, including South African artists, such as Gavin Jantjes, who are struggling to live in Europe, struggling to get recognition, and trying to contact other artists from the Third World. Their interest is in other Third World art and artists. Oguibe has been drawing from Australian Aboriginal material. He saw a Fante flag exhibit, and now he draws from Fante flag designs. It is a sort of internationalism where a Third World artist draws from the art of other Third

World people. Several artists in Nsukka are drawing from other cultures too. Ndidi Dike, for instance, uses little brass figures from other parts of West Africa.

I have talked to Bruce Onobrakpeya about this, and I think I agree with him. His argument is you have to have a strong cultural base from which you are operating. From that base, you can go out and either draw or refuse to draw from other cultures. You can take, mix styles, invent new ones, or reinvent old styles. But without a cultural base, you're lost. It may be that some of the African artists in England or Europe and America are in danger of losing their cultural base like American artists in Paris, such as Mary Cassatt in the 1930s, or American writers, for that matter who saw Paris as a mecca and who became sort of pseudo-French for a while, being very much influenced by French literature. This attitude contrasts with that of a few writers, such as Hemingway, who kept on writing in the typical American style.

Nigerian artists want more contact with the rest of the world, and this is very difficult now because of the economic situation in the country. At the same time, they are occupied with social and political conditions here. Too much internationalism tends to pull them away from that kind of thing. But I think internationalism will increase. There is no doubt about it that external influences are going to increase although I do not think it is leading to one world culture. I think the distinction will deepen absolutely. In fact, they seem to be reinforcing rather than disappearing.

GR: In spite of the vibrant developments in modern art in Nigeria, which you reported in a ACASA newsletter (1993), it is still disheartening that much of Western patronage and scholarship glosses over this fact with their insistence on the authenticity to art forms that court the interest of the auction houses, collectors, and gloss exhibition catalogs. There is this apparent reluctance by the West to recognize the existence of modern art in Africa.

Ottenberg: Either they say it is derivative of Europe or they say that it is folksy with all those masquerades dancing around. Anthropologists have not been that much interested in contemporary Third World art until recently, and the interest has come rather indirectly through touristic naïvety or popular art, the kind of thing Middle Art (Augustine Okoye) does. Such art is interesting. I love to see it, and I have bought a couple of his works, but it does have some kind of kitschy quality to it. They are produced by artists who are not artists in a technical sense.

Western art historians are terribly arrogant about the West. They are very Eurocentric, and this is tied to an older view of evolution of human culture in which the modernist period in the West is the high point of this cultural evolution. These assumptions, however, are breaking down in the postmodernist period, the age of multiculturalism making pastiches of the so called Third World and other non-Western cultures while insisting on defining the resulting cultural mélange in its own terms, its own paradigms.

There is a lot of writing going on in Europe. I was recently reading something that was written a few years ago, in the Netherlands, and I was surprised to hear the same arguments in England at the INIVA Conference, as well as in America. Multiculturalism, which suggests that there is no one best culture, is increasingly enhanced by tremendous migration, improved communication, the CNN phenomenon, and the breaking down of nation-states because of multinational businesses. States are losing control of their economies, and as all these things are going on, they suggest a loosening up—a much better situation for the Third and Fourth World who themselves are now making more demands and beginning to come together in large groups. But there is a sort of idealistic gloat over this multiculturalism. The fact is economic power still remains with Europe and America, and now Japan and China are coming up, and that's going to be the decider on the direction of art and cultural discourses in the ultimate sense. I don't share the optimism that some individuals have.

There are substantial shifts, but they are coming very slowly. The Smithsonian National Museum of African Art in Washington DC is nowhere committed to exhibiting contemporary art on a regular basis. It is going to have an exhibit of African artists living in the United States. It may be easier to put such exhibits together, but it is more difficult for me to find pieces in Nigeria and make arrangements to get them to the United States.

In Europe, contemporary African art is better received in the continent than in England. I talked to the owner of Savannah

Gallery in London, Leroi Coubagy, sometime ago. I asked who buys from you, and he said they are mostly Italians and Germans. I inquired about the British and Americans, and he said the British practically never buy from them while only a few regular Americans visit the gallery. For the Nsukka group, there was a strong, long history of relationship with Germany, which goes back to the Nigerian Civil War, when Uche Okeke exiled himself to raise political support for Biafra and exhibited young artists from Biafra there. Obiora Udechukwu, Tayo Adenaike, and Tony Uwachukwu have shown up in Germany and were well received.

GR: The contribution any scholar, African or outsider, can make to contemporary art from Africa would be to shift focus to the present unfolding art experience rather than this insistence on celebrating the arts of precolonial Africa?

Ottenberg: There have been a number of general exhibits that have covered contemporary African art. There was one in Paris, Magiciens de la Terre, in 1989. There was Africa Hoy, and there was Primitivism in 20th Century Art in 1984, and Africa Explores, which Susan Vogal curated. All of these were general in nature.

GR: But in these major exhibits you cited, there is always the temptation to show what you earlier described as kitschy art. Take the constructions of Kane Kwei, and the painting of Cheri Samba in Magiciens and in Africa Explores.

Ottenberg: Sure. Imagine an art exhibit having the little Magicians of the Earth! These artists are identified first as magicians and conjurers, not as artists. Why weren't they artists of the earth?

GR: What we are seeing is probably a remnant of the stereotypical but now generally faulted image of the African artists as a ritualist, a religious image maker.

Ottenberg: It is undergoing a transition. There was this Dutch symposium that I was reading about. The big question was where do you show Contemporary Third World Art? Do you show it in an ethnological or an art museum? There was a tremendous argument, but the final conclusion was that it was all right to show both in so far as the little differences are shown. In the anthropology museum, the exhibit may show a little more cultural background material while in the art museum, aesthetics, and styles are emphasized. But look, to me what is needed is what I am trying to do. We have had enough general exhibits. We now need specific, detailed scholarly studies of groups of artists or of single artists and their works. We need to take individual artists, or a group of artists, to show the kind of stylistic changes or changes in images that they have gone through over time. We need to do that kind of basic work. There are very few detailed studies of contemporary art. There is a lot of literature, but most of it is very thin. You even see it in Jean Kennedy's book, which I admire very much because she has pulled together a lot of data, even if a lot of it is surface studies. There are good descriptions there but not much analysis. It is a very good reference work. But I am not saying all these things because I am an anthropologist. Nor am I suggesting anthropologists are the ones to do this kind of work. Art historians and artists themselves who are interested should be very much involved in these studies. I am talking about art history and anthropology, each one has the skills that the other lacks. I lack a thorough knowledge of European art history and it hampers my work.

GR: And this blocks your analytical sensitivities? Ottenberg: I have to struggle with it. I am trying not to block myself. I read very carefully what others say about style and technique, and then I try to understand the language of analysis. On the other hand, people in art history may lack the sensitivities and understanding of cultures and cultural processes that I have. GR: It is disheartening that we have our own art historians, several in America and elsewhere, yet we are not getting from them the kind of responses that you recommend. If they thought what you advocate is worthwhile, we probably would not need to have you engage in this project in spite of the odds, in spite of your handicaps.

Ottenberg: I think it is coming. I have met some younger people, graduate students at the Smithsonian who are interested in doing some work on contemporary African art.

Printed in the United States
by Baker & Taylor Publisher Services